THE STORY OF THE EXXON VALDEZ

Time Travel History with Tracy Jeanette and The Gang

Turk Allcott

TAe Books
A Division of Turk Allcott Enterprises

ISBN: 978-1-300-00023-5

Cover art and internal gifs: Animation Factory

The Story of The Exxon Valdez
March 24, 1989

First, you need some background of the year 1989. Which was a real year in ancient history. Know what? I think I'll make these reference points of background into a table on every history adventure, so you can fit in, like we did.

THE YEAR … 1989

Clothes stylings	Sneakers way retro. Torn jeans. And leg warmers.
Hair style	Do-your-own-thing. Which means mess-up is ok. Oh, and nerd looks, too.
Cool ways to act	Chew gum. Play Pac Man (an ancient video game, which I learned as prep-work).
Food sources	Taco Bell and Skittles. McDonald's of course, duh.
Music to know	This dirty dancing (it's ok, don't freak) song to hum, of Hungry Eyes, of scoping someone royal.

Turk's Introduction

Can you learn History from a time-traveling ten year old? Sure, I guess. But the real question is, should you? I mean, is it just too embarrassing or de-meaning, sifting through a young person's viewpoint just to get at a few facts?

I don't know.

Hey, wait! It's fun, the fun way to do things. That's the way I like to learn, the fun way. But you might be different.

Anyway, it's all moot. I'm incapable of professional writing. So I'll just stick to editing and leave the creative stuff to a real writer, even though she's only ten. Tracy Jeanette.

Good Reading,

Always, Turk Allcott

Professional Introduction

First, I'm Tracy Jeanette and I'm ten, duh. You know me from bigtime adventures like *Time Leak* and others. Oh, and my editor godfather is Mr. Allcott who helped handle the busy work of assemblage of these stories, but enough of that cuz it's way boring. Not you, Mr. Allcott! I mean the stupid process of after-afflecks of writing and so forth.

Okay. Anyway, about the first of these history lesson fun adventure stories.

One week in spring I had a report due on the environment. Which…oh, I forgot to mention . . . I'm home-schooled. For now. Next year I go to Parkview, which is a real school with brick walls and professional teachers. And principals. So everything I learn there will be real. For sure!

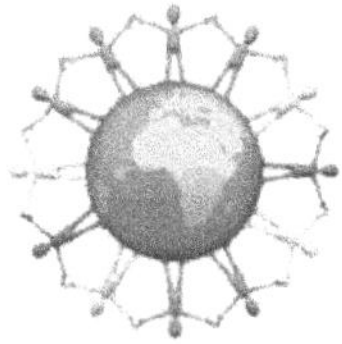

Anyway, Mom made me do a report on the environment, anything I wanted within environmental limits, and of course Dad cracked a dumb joke cuz he's a way renegade, unlike Mom, and he said:

"Do one on Global Warming. Go to the library and look under science fiction."

Stupid. He always rumbles on about gas and seatbelts and cell phones and helmets and youth-a-nazya and other stuff out of the blue. But then he doesn't care, cuz he just goes off singing and planning another golf vacation. Which Mom just sniffs at.

So I thought: hmmm. Environment. Which first I wasn't sure what that meant. So I looked it up and it meant EVERYTHING! Luckies! The board was wide open. Then I thought: hmmm. The ground floor of environment--dirt. And not just natural kind, that's probably what you're thinking of right now. No. *Unnatural* dirt. And then I thought of a spill. Like one you can't hide, you know, unlike a dinner spill of a couple rice bits which you just slip under your jean legs on the sly or like that. But no. How about a gigantic spill? Was more my thought. One which you get totally blamed for cuz it's out in the open.

So I was room-innating on that concept down in the Big Field when the Old Man popped in. Who I've told you is totally Arnold and younged up now, with even a girl friend!, gag me to the moon. Only luckily she's Sklo, who we like. The former Mad Ham Curing of also Maria Sklodowska.

"Vatt's ubb?" the Old Man asked me.

"Hi. We're sitting here thinking of spills." I had Tosci the mouse with me. And Maggie Duck and Maurice the robin.

"Ja, like ze Valdeeze."

We nodded. Only we didn't know valdeez, which maybe that was a joke or something. Luckily, or as the Old Man sometimes says, randomly, J.T. Woodchuck wandered by then and he stretched and rolled around and dirted up and then asked:

"Bad sneeze?"

"Nine. Valdeeze. Ze oil sbill."

Well that was good news! Cuz oil is environment of the dark side and there was a spill involved, too! Omg. So I told the Old Man about my homework and he said:

"Vee coult do a hisdory tribb."

And that's how it all started. The Old Man used his time watchy and a group of us made that first history trip. To which I found out it's Exxon Valdez, spelled like that. Better get the spelling right if you want full credit!

Later, we took even more trips. Way more, for more learning. But this was the first, and here was, were, the rules, laid down by the Old Man.

IMPORTANT RULES OF HISTORY TRAVELING
From the Old Man, which I will translate

1. We cannot change the history. Of like trying to fix certain element things. Cuz that will have ram-if-face-shuns of actually wrecking stuff on accident. Go figure!
2. We *can*, can, talk to people and mingle around and hang out, but the Old Man has to check afterwards if we wrecked anything, just by talking. If we did, we weren't in trouble. But he would wipe the slate clean. Actually, he said: "I vill negade ze tribb vissin ze Planck-Heisenberg barameters." So that was good news! And we all said yayy!
3. When possible, we should only talk to animal friends, of that time period. Which Fat Charlie Chipmunk objected: "Yeah? They're all primitive idiots. They don't talk." And he was right, thinking about earlier adventures. Animals tend not to talk. For the most part. But the Old Man said he had a trick or two up his sleeve. Something about reconstitute, not milk, but Big Field properties. So it's okay.
4. Only a few of my friends can go on each trip, maybe two or three. Or maybe four. Cuz the Old Man said he didn't want a

headache of juggling too many extra body timelines. Whatever that means!

Okay. Anyway, here comes our first history trip. It was fun. But kind of a tragedy which is as you'll see. So I guess we have to live with it. Us survivors.

Booking the Crew

For this history lesson travel crew, we had a conference in the Big Field and selected the following travelers:

Tosci the mouse, pronounced Toss-Key, who is a sensitive person-animal of no insensitivity, caring but fun and a sidekick of…

Fat Charlie Chipmunk, who is total fun but insensitive to the nth. A bad influence a few times.

Folder Fox, askerbick wit of being smart, almost as smart as his twin brother Titus, but a touch tone nicer.

Me. Duh. Which this picture is me babed up after that Time Leak adventure. My favorite.

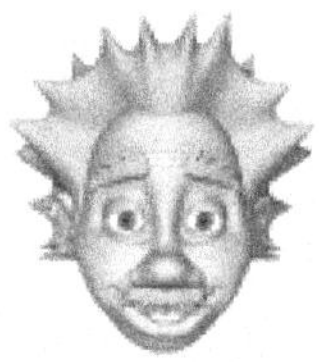

The Old Man before he younged up and was still yuro and famous. Before he died in 1955. You can see why we called him the Old Man! Back then I mean.

We had a couple days of prebaration, as the Old Man says. So I learned of being a 1989-ite. And we got the rules of the land and a little of what to expect. A kind of summary history from the Old Man, who had popped back there in that distant world to scout it out.

It turned out we would be in Alaska territory, which is cold and white, even the bears, which we know one local bear who pops in now and then but he's brown. His name is Carl and he talks, cuz of our Big Field properties of Lo-Jistic or something. Anyway, Carl said if he moved to Alaska he would have to evolve to white fur which he wasn't sure of how to do it. He told us his brown fur would stand out, and not in a good way. Something about nature being unforgiving, so we concluded of peer pressure, even in the wild.

Okay. So on D-Day, departure day, we had our dress . . . not rehearsal . . . but launching. And us travelers gathered together and all the others inched back and then the Old Man adjusted his gold watchy up on his forearm,way buff now!, and poof! Off we went. Through time and space.

Onboard the Exxon Valdez

Right onto a big oil tanker ship! Cold as Alaska at midnight. Which it was almost.

The wind was whistling through a crack in the rubber lining part of a door. We were inside this sort of stupid room with a couple steel chairs and some big folders and an ugly green table and no window. We peeked around the door opening. There was a narrow hall and some stairs up to outside.

"Amit-chips," the Old Man told us. "Vell, of ze zuperstrructure. Vich is in ze back, like ze Corvette, ja?" Which meant something. He checked his watch. "Eleffen sirty. We haff half un hour. Vant to scoud arount?"

We all said way yeah.

"Bull ubb your coad."

Which I bundled way up my sheep-collar overcoat. Now to over the top of my underneath stealth jacket, set to seventy four degrees, a little high cuz of the Alaska. But that stealth jacket was an Old Man gift from the future, so I had to keep it hidden under normal artificial clothes.

None of the boys had any clothes whatsoever, like *ever*, cuz they're fur-bearing wear-your-own. With no animal rights violation. So don't try spray-painting their backs when they're not looking.

We walked up the metal holey stairs and . . .

Okay, here coming up is a picture of our tanker, kind of, which I ripped off, I mean borrowed from wikipedia for extra credit.

[I asked Mr. Allcott, of stealing this picture, you know, cuz of plague-urisms and such and he said:

"Go ahead. What are they going to do, sue us?" And then he laughed at something. Dumb.]

Oil tanker (side view)

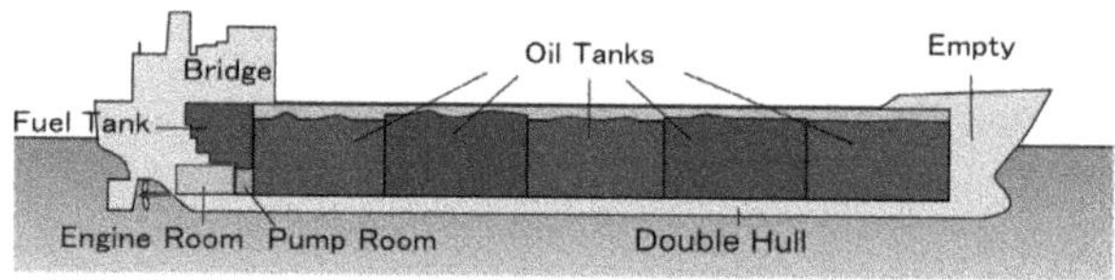

Anyway, we made a once-around on this next level up in the Bridge part, seeing nothing. Then this guy came down the next higher stairwell. A smaller like a port-a-gee type guy like Dad's gardener now that we have one. Every week on Tuesday.

"Howty!" introduced the Old Man.

That port-a-gee guy, he gave us a way strange look, like what-are-you-doing up at this time of night and how-come you're on my ship. Which I helped out.

"It's not bedtime at our place," I told him. "Plus, this is just a visit. For a history assignment."

Know what? That guy never said a word. But he did scribble a note in some flip book like I was in major dutch, so I was a little nervous. Duh. The Old Man patted that guy on the shoulder, though, for calmness. Who just shook his head and kept going downstairs.

"Propably checking ze tanks," the Old Man told us. "Tanks stretch all ze way to ze front, a number of them." [As you can see by the cool drawing]. "Und zey haff senssors, zo he can make sure they're all rrright."

We got it. Bigtime. Tanks full of crude oil, which we had pre-knowledge about. Crude is not like rude or gross. Just oil which is not ready for primetime, for your gas tank. They have to massage it for that. Put in stuff. Or take stuff out. I forget.

"How many of these working morons are on the ship?" Folder Fox wanted to know, about the oiltanker crew.

"Oh, tventy-fife or zo. It's ze VLCC."

"Come again?" asked Folder Fox again.

"Verrry Larch Grude Garrier. Sdate of ze ard. Before ze ULCC und more double hulls. Brompted by ziss accident."

We all nodded, way understanding Grude, which is Old Man talk for crude. The rest was secondary information which we deposited in our wait-till-we-need-it brain cells.

"Let's jeck out Kagan!" the Old Man enthused. "But be quiedd. Vee don't want to wake him."

Kagan was a guy who was a stand-in pilot of steering this here craft, matey. Yo ho. Which Charlie Chipmunk does that impression better than me. Sorry.

"Dude's bagging some zzz's?" asked Charlie.

"Ssshh!" said the Old Man.

We stealthed up to the pilot room and stared through the doorway and there Kagan was, conked in his chair, head over on one arm side. The Old Man told Folder Fox:

"Pudd on Dracy's chacket."

Which I took off my stealth jacket and handed it over.

"Now," the Old Man told Folder Fox, who had my jacket on and turned on the stealth mode and was all invisible. From that future technology I told you about. Before. Oh, wrong book. Anyway, the Old Man said:

"Zneak in zere und put in ze buck."

"We tipping this guy?" wondered Folder Fox, probably scratching his head. "I thought he wrecked it."

"No. Buck. Buck. Organigg device."

I got it first.

"Bug!" I exclaimed. "Spy bug, for listening!" And the Old Man backed me up.

"Ja. Vuture teggnology, viss video. Twelve hour livezpan. Pudd it in a good spodd. You know vatt to do."

And the Old Man gave Folder this fly-looking thing which was cool but not a real fly. Unless it was dead. But even then, still not a fly.

"Check it out!" liked Charlie Chipmunk of that thing. "Cool for a salad trick. Freak your guest. Does it move? Simulate activity maybe?"

"No," said the Old Man.

So we waited while Folder Fox sneaked in that spy thing and when he finally came back and gave me back my jacket, the Old Man sprung a new one on us. He said come this way, not sounding exactly like Arnold but close, and we went back down one level and over to a window area. And then he broke out chairs, those galaxy ones which human velcroe you in without seat belts. The Old Man turned on an air computer, like a holo-vision one, and we saw Robert Kagan dozing in the pilot house just like he was right in front of us.

"Dude had a shot of scotch whiskey next to him," Folder Fox told us. "See that glass? I took a nip."

"Part-ay!" liked Fat Charlie Chipmunk, wanting maybe even to hustle back and try some himself.

"Hokay, vait," the Old Man told us. He checked his watch, using it for time-checking only this time, not traveling. "Eleffen fifty fife. Nine minudes."

Charlie had to sing to that. Duh.

"I'm gonna wait! Till the midnight hour! When my love comes tumb--"

"Ssssh! Jarlie! Chust relax."

We had like nine minutes until lift-off, or not, which is a huge timelength. Where you can get bored beyond Rangoon. Luckily we started an eye spy, which Tosci the mouse always likes. Charlie was first up on spying and Tosci did the first question bank.

"Is it white?" asked Tosci.

"Nope," said Charlie Chipmunk.

“Is it big?”

“No.”

“Is it a person?”

“Nope.”

“Is it moving?”

“Nope.”

Well that went on for a bunch of nopes until the Old Man said hang on, which then Charlie spilled the beans about he was eyeballing a star, up in the sky, duh.

“That’s white!” objected Tosci. “And big! And even moving--”

But he couldn’t finish on the objection machine cuz we rocked the boat, baby. Bigtime.

Crash! Boom! Bam!

"Crrrrunch!"

Our chairs jiggled around in a major fashion way and then we got throwed, threw, maybe thrown, I don't know, but we were lucky to be velcroed cuz wow! Talk about a whiplash! That VLCC came to a screeching halt!

"Ze Ply Reef!" exclaimed the Old Man.

Charlie and us, we, dug all the rock and roll. To the nth. Baby. Which was the highlight of this adventure. Charlie praised Robert Kagan, our control driver:

"This guy rules!"

Then we watched the holo-screen cuz Kagan was getting totally jumped on by these two guys on intercom, which I got their names later. Chief mate or maybe firstmate James Kunkel and Captain Joseph Hazelwood. I got those names totally right later, from a newspaper at the hotel. Which I'll get to. Later.

First the Firstmate (duh!) chimed in, over the radio:

"What in the bloody name of Jesus happened!"

"Bligh Reef, sir," answered Kagan, maybe trying to blame it on another guy. Which was a good try but like no soap. Cuz even I knew of Captain Bligh of history and also that Tahiti movie. And he was way dead.

Know what? I later found out Kagan meant it was the Bligh *reef* which was not a guy. It was just land. In the ocean! Go figure. And Kagan ran into it. Like Mom did of that Honda bike which was hidden behind our car as we left the dry cleaners and then she tried to prop it back up, which she did cuz she's pretty strong, and then we paced around and had to leave a note cuz nobody came racing out or cared.

Anyway, I'll tell you more about reefs later. FYI cool nature junk.

"Get the harbor master."

So now a third person came over on the radio.

We watched Kagan on our screen. He was still alone and totally sweating up bullets and puttering back and forth, peering over both sides of the room. Once he almost mad arm-swiped our bug, which had me worried, but then I saw he was just punching the air of an invisible assassin. Ninja practice.

Captain Hazelwood said:

"I'm on my way! What does harbor say?"

Harbor told Kagan to steer off, which he tried I guess. Then firstmate Kunkel yelled at him:

"You're understeering! Port! Port!"

Which Fat Charlie Chipmunk cheered for some reason. Tosci the mouse later whispered to me that Charlie told him Port is wine and maybe a toga party or something was in the works, which was a no-go.

Cuz now the tanker was totally stuck on Bligh Reef.

We absorbed the action for way too much of a more while, and there was a bunch of running on stairways and Captain Hazelwood came onto the bridge and then the firstmate, and then others, in a non-stop parade of one-zees and two-zees, and then the Old Man told us:

"Zot's it. Let's hit a hotel und scoud oud ze damage in ze morning."

"Pop back here in the forecastle?" asked Folder Fox, majorly swank-talking sailor jibe or jibberish.

"Nine. No," said the Old Man. "Vee take ze heliggopter!"

And we all cheered.

The Oil Spill

Guess where we stayed that night? Homer! Ha ha, just like the Simpsons, doh! Only this was an Alaska town. With a hotel.

We could have future-jumped, but the Old Man said once we occupied this timeline it was better to minimize jumps. For some reason. Way technical I'm sure. He said maybe only once. So save your timeouts.

We score-got this kind of scummy, sorries, five star room--NOT--which was over the top noisy, mostly from us test-jumping the beds, but also other people in other rooms talking and snoring. Luckily we all nodded off in like five minutes. After a late night snack of Cheeze-Its and no Red Bull.

In the morning we bundled up bigtime and the landlady downstairs said we needed a hearty meal before sightseeing, only I don't think she was a landlady exactly, not sure, maybe rent-a-lady. That type.

So we scarfed bacon and eggs and biscuits and gravy and french toast and hot chocolate, the guys sneaking out of pocket for a load up, including Folder Fox who was stealthed in a chair next to us.

And it looked way freaky when a big piece of bacon floated off the table and disappeared. Once even the landlady saw it. She gave us directions to the helicopter place. Then she peered at the air food.

"Machick," the Old Man explained, about the floating bacon. He nodded to her and grinned.

She smiled back a huge one and then sashayed away, not believing anymore in disappearing bacon.

"Hokay," pronounced the Old Man when we were done. "Ledds roll!"

Ready for us outside was a dark gray Ford-350 superduty megatruck. Charlie Chipmunk gave Tosci the mouse an elbow nudge. Tosci nodded back. Charlie a lot of times thinks the Old Man has Terminator Tendencies. Probably cuz of his voice and now buffness.

"You need a pair of shades," Charlie told him. "Cap off the image."

"Idds not bright out."

"Could get that way later. And we'll be up in the chopper."

"Ja, I sink your rrright. Chust a minude."

He took Charlie with him and we waited while the two of them hit the gift shop back inside. When they came out, Charlie had on a kid's pair with green border lines, and the Old Man had, duh, a pair

Charlie picked out for him which were black and wraparound.

"Off vee go!" and the Old Man crammed it into gear with a gravel crunch pullout.

Get this. The Old Man rented the helicopter by himself. No pilot. Which, let me explain for you newbies. The Old Man is way schooled in all tecky stuff now, and he has licenses for everything. Plus, he can get cash on emergencies. Which, not thinking bad thoughts, he usually pays back, from knowing stuff. Anyway, maybe he even bought that helicopter temporarily, I don't know.

So we took off. Up in the whirly-bird eggbeater chopper. Lifting off in super noise mode wreck-your-ear-hairs, I mean permanently, if you weren't prepared. But we were. Note. Bigtime. See next paragraph, for all the HTH.

We sportated mini-pod communicators, not cover-your-head Magnum PI ones like that stupid show Dad likes. Of TC always yelling when they're up in the air. Our ear pods were designer and small from the future. No yelling necessary. The Old Man described the origin maker manufacturer of that probably bailout company of the future:

"Ja. From ze year 2157. By Fermigant. Noice rrreducing und localizing VR. You dick zem?"

"Cool, very cool," agreed Folder Fox. "But, and this is important, you keep saying dick-it and dick-this and like that. You can't do that. It's DIG them, not dick them. Try it."

“Dickgg zem.”

“Again.”

And they worked on English all the way to over Prince William Sound.

It was okay visible that morning and we finally caught sight of our tanker, the VLCC one. The spilly one from this lesson. Oh yeah, Exxon Valdez. Dummies! Got to remember that for my report. Exxon Valdez. Okay.

The Exxon Valdez was stopped. Cold. Duh. All around it, on the front end, was a mega blotch of oil floating on the water doing nothing. On the port side, that’s the left, there were super long streaks, starting narrow and then widening out. The rest of the sound water was super clear. Except in the blotch and oil streak zones.

“Zee it?” the Old Man instructed us. We all answered no-like-we’re-blind, get a clue.

And here following is a map of the area zoom in and zoom out and of the day mark-up of the spill rate (complicated!) which I ripped off, I mean claimed, from a picture site from somewhere. Who cares? Anyway, study it if you want to. I'm sure it's cool in some sort of way.

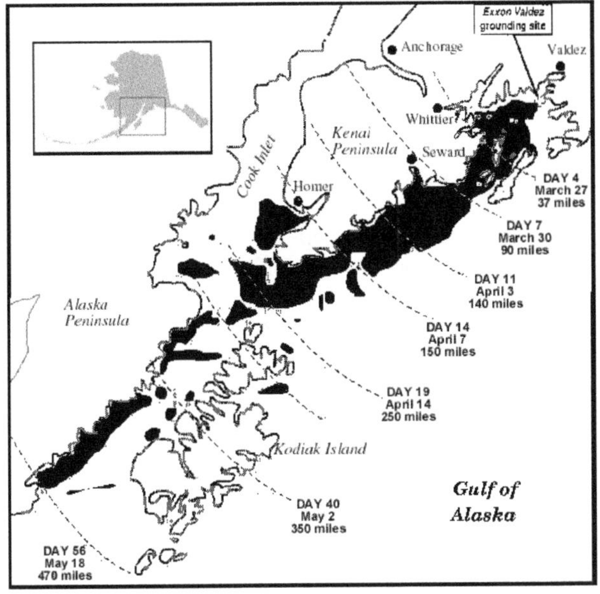

"Eleffen million gallons," the Old Man was instructing. "Of ze oil. Vurst sbill in history. Check it out while I zircle arount. Dickgg it."

"Cool!" agreed Fat Charlie Chipmunk.

"It's not cool," said Tosci the mouse. "That's a huge mess."

"Not hurting anyone," countered Charlie, who is definitely not mess-a-phobic. Just check out his home sometime.

"Oil on water isn't natural," went on Tosci the mouse. "Right?" He wanted support from the Old Man.

"Yes und No," he supported, kind of.

"YES!" enthused Fat Charlie Chipmunk, who likes half answers.

"Oil zeeps," continued the Old Man as we manoovered one more banker-leaner get-ready-to-puke- royal turn. "Oil zeeps up vrom ze zea bottom und . . . you know vatt oil iss?"

Oops. Science time. That's the Old Man for you. He thinks his science lessons add way fun to adventures. Which we only partly do.

More About Oil

Down below, a tractor tugboat was roaming around, getting ready for non-dirt activities of the water kind. I think yanking and pushing. Go to timeout kid stuff.

"Oil," answered Folder Fox, who is the most science among us, but not as good as his twin brother Titus Fox, who reads *Scientific American* throw-outs from Mr. Hallocatt's dumpster. Anyway Folder continued in a super confident extra-credit voice:

"Oil is both glue, sticky . . . and it's smooth, like lotion. It's made out of plastic. Except molten. A liquid. Liquid plastic."

We all nodded. Except the Old Man.

"No. Nine."

Nine is an additional NO, from the Old Man. Nine is his former science language, which science uses numbers.

Folder Fox acted shocked at a wrong answer.

But I could tell he was not shocked, in reality. Not from his slight not-narrow eye look. And then, lightbulb thoughts! I concluded Folder Fox had been bluffing with his oil answers. Like when he tells you he has a big flush draw but he really has two pair or a set and he wants you to call.

"What is it then?" quiz backed Folder Fox, like the Old Man didn't know either about oil specifics and would have to bluff too.

"Vell, zere are all kinds of ze oil of course, bessides betroleum--"

"Yo ho, yo ho!" Charlie Chipmunk contributed. Which I know what he was thinking, and so did the Old Man. Since we were over the ocean and boats.

"Ja. Ze Whale oil. You like zat vun?"

"Duh," answered Charlie. And Tosci the mouse also answered yes he did very much.

"Whale oil," instructed the Old Man, vass bick in ze 1800's. Und before. Idd gums from blubber. From ze *Eubalalena japonica*."

We gave him a look about obese whales and babies and Japan but he added: "Vrum ze Right Whale."

"Naturally," added Charlie, "not the Wrong Whale." Charlie gave Tosci a high five.

"Und eeffen more important, ze Sperm Whale."

Well you can imagine then I turned almost color-me-red. Folder Fox smirked me with an eyebrow raise. Tosci the mouse just did a tsk-tsk.

“Ja,” continued the Old Man. “You can gedd tons out of a Sperm Whale’s head. Vich idd’s a wax. From zat you melt it und gedd oil for candles. Und eefen gozmedics. Und butter . . . vell, margarine.”

Luckily the Old Man turned his attention from sex type whale oil to normal oil, the start-your-car kind.

“Anyvay, vee don’t neet whale oil any more. Zooo . . . Save ze Whale!”

And we all okayed dat. But not really excited about saving a fish, which they’re only TV stars. Folder Fox nodded and definated our point of view:

“CYA. Just in case.”

We all knew from Star Trek and other sources, do a good deed and if the tables are turned maybe some day the whales will save us, if the case may be.

“As I sssaid,” continued the Old Man, “ze oil, betroleum, zeeps nadurally out of ze zea bottom. Und makes tar on ze beaches, like in Galifornia. Surfs ubb, dute! Und, gedd ziss, betroleum oil gumms from dinosaurs!”

Of course we wanted to get excited about that, about dinosaurs being added into the equation. But we were on red alert for a joke. I mean, we’re not marks. Which means suckers or shills or Georges--all terms we get from the Fox boys, among others--

which means just dumb. So we waited for the joke. Finally Charlie said for us:

“Come ON!”

“No, idds true.”

“Dinosaurs? In the ocean?”

“Vell, ok. Also fish. Und blankton. Anyvay . . . ze fishes are smashed under ze zea und after a long dime . . . you gedd oil!”

“So,” explained Folder Fox for us, hopefully putting the finishing ribbon around study hour, “you just dig up the fish guts and pour them into your Chevy. Easy peasy.”

“Vell . . . nodd zo zimple. Ze hydrocarbons haff to be broken apard, vractional distillation, und zen . . .”

But, got to be honest, we tuned out the Old Man then. Too busy.

Down below a bunch of guys were up on deck on the Exxon Valdez--got it!--and others were up on that pusher tug and everyone was yelling at each other, which we could tell by the arm waves. That tug tried to knock over the tanker boat, which was defenseless, so it was a not-fair war, but anyway nothing happened. We waited for another contest but no dice.

Later when we pulled away, Charlie asked:

"Why don't they just clear out and light it all up?"

Which Tosci the mouse pooh-poohed, but I could tell by his eye highlights he was hoping for that excitement. As were we all. I mean, so say we all.

"No. Zat danker is vorth too much. Und zat would kill ze odders und fish."

Sorries.

"They could just let it dissolve," tried Tosci.

"No. Oil doesn't mix viss ze vater. Idd iss hydrophobic."

Charlie started singing the Old Yeller song, which I own that old Disney one.

None of us joined in, cuz even Folder Fox admits a tear comes out of your eye when you just think of it and don't even have a dog yet but want one. Can you say Christmas present? Luckily the Old Man provided our last agenda. Of this history lesson.

"Eeffen after cleaning ziss mess ubb, a lot of animals vere killed. Vich I'll show you neggst. To rrrap ziss up.

"Dickggck it!" he tried one more time, and we jetted coptered away from the scene of the crime.

After lunch--a super BLT with a hot chocolate (very kind of yucky gloopy into conjeel bloops, I think it was instance type)--we time-jumped forward to one more stop. One year later, March 4, 1990. Another real year in ancient history. The last stop in our trip to Exxon Valdez Alaska in that crazy earlier past century.

We Meet Riki and Mike

It was only eight in the morning. Nobody was around except for a lady girl with red hair and a red face and a long black wooly coat. She came up to us as we rounded around this stand-up pool.

"Hello, there!"

"Howty," answered the Old Man.

"Going to the celebration? You're early!"

That's when I helped:

"It's way early. Like hours before the last stop."

She just laughed and said remember, noon on the dot. And they had trucks if we needed a ride. I whispered to the Old Man to put on his shades to show her we didn't need one. Then we said thanks and she went off into a breakfast building is my guess.

"If she only knew," I said to the Old Man in a very cool tone, and he elbow-nudged me. The boys abandoned pocket-ship and roamed free and the Old Man told us:

"Ziss iss Kamechak Bay, rehab. For ze odders und birds."

We knew of rehab, cuz of *In Touch* mag, about Lindsey and others, like Mary Kate and Iron Man. Folder Fox told us all:

"Plays havoc with a marriage."

Which I agreed with, for normal people. Except Hollywood types are supposed to have more than one marriage, usually, so don your excuses as you may. Charlie Chipmunk, as usual!, got to the root rot of the issue:

"Whose dealing to these guys?"

Well, that started a whole debate among us visitors, including yours truly, about whether you could stop bird-dealing and otter-dealing without getting at the underneath issues. But the Old Man interrupted us:

"Over here! I'll try my deffice."

And he used a flash memory silver thing which did a light spray around the pool tank and these two clean otters flopped up on the ledge and addressed us:

"Hello," said one otter.

"I'm Riki, this here is Mike," said the other. Both had nice Canadian voices. Folder Fox introduced our end of the equation.

"And this is the Old Man," I added.

They both eyeballed the Old Man with twisty heads and whiskers twitching and he bowed way low. Very cool.

"You rrreddy to be frree?" he asked them.

"I *thought* that was on the agenda." said Riki. "Who are you, ay, the head honcho?"

"No."

Mike the other otter said: "Don't really care who it is. Glad for anyone to pull us out of this tank. Sick and tired of all the scrubbing and cooing and patronising."

The Old Man explained to us:

"Marine workers proffided ziss refuge und cleaned off all ze oil und monitored zese greatures. Ferry exbensive. Over ten sousand per odder."

"Money is no object," said Mike. "Greater good and all that."

Riki added: "How'd *you* like to be caked in oil, ay? Say goodbye to that fancy jacket. And pants."

"And shoes," added Mike. "Ay, you hear the one about the husband who put in a new carpet for his wife, then stepped out for a smoke?"

We said no and I said I don't smoke yet and hopefully never but Mike the otter went on:

"Can't find his sigs, ay, so he goes back inside and sees a lump under the carpet. Not worth pulling it all up and starting over, so he takes a hammer and mashes it down good till it's okey dokey. Just then his wife comes in and says: "Found your smokes, here they are. Now if I can just find the parakeet."

The Old Man only, he guffawed at that sick joke, the rest of us grimmered politely. A couple of seagulls pop squawked in high voices from an aviary that was off toward the far side of the Kamechak Bay clean-up zone:

"Leave off the bird jokes, ay?"

"Or what," replied Mike the otter. "Five for pecking?"

"All because of that darned reef," remanissed Riki. "And that rookie helmsman."

"Wasn't a rookie, just incompetent," added Mike.

"Hey," said Mike. "Want to see a shot of us in our oil coats?"

We said sure and he hustled over and back and gave us this one which he let me keep. He said he could always get another copy from the Anchorage News if he needed it. At cocktail parties probably.

“Anyway,” said Riki. “Totally incompetent. Who can miss the Bligh Reef? I mean, not miss it, hit it by accident. Biggest watermark in the Sound. What a boob!”

“You still,” said Fat Charlie Chipmunk to those two now-clean guys, “dwelling about reefers, this close to getting out of rehab? Lay off the drugs.”

“Stunt your growth,” added Folder Fox. Tosci the mouse nodded.

“Oh, these boys are cards, ay?” boomed Mike way out loud.

The Old Man then said, mostly to us visitors:

“Hokay. Ply Reef is ze cold water goral reef. Idds made ubb of goral bolyps, billions of tiny animals, in ze ocean. Mostly galcium garbonate.”

Now I remembered. From my personal family Hawaii trip and that Hana Uma Mow Mow snorkel place where they make you watch a stupid movie to get in and then when you snorkel like way outside like Dad always goad-ates us to, but Mom hates and says she won't, you could get scatched by that coral rock. Which I guess is non-moving animals. Of some type.

"Ledds vait it out inside. Vith zum more hot chocolate. Hokay?"

And we all said yaw and goodbye to the Riki and Mike show and those dumb seagulls and we headed inside to way better hot cocoa with whipped cream.

At noon a big crowd of us trucked over to the Sound.

That's the name of their ocean part. Sound. Dumb.

It was okay outside, now. Which didn't matter cuz I was toasty at seventy two degrees on my jacket set-up. Toast toast. There was a band and a talk--way boring--about our part in the Earth universe of how we were bad but we had a duty to protect other creatures and some other stuff which I tuned out cuz Tosci and I were hogging the peanuts from Charlie for a twist of fate see how *you* like it.

Then the band started up and a major truck pulled close to the water and Riki and Mike, not talking now, they got let out and they flapped over into the ice cold water it looked like, and they were off.

The band played *Off We Go*, which is an Air Force song not water-based, so was totally stupid, but anyway . . . know what? This is an R-rated part coming up, so turn away for just a second.

You don't want to know this next part. But I have to. For poss tearity. Plus, good reporters have to record the bad as well as the normal. Future generations might not have our sensibilities and things change.

To which Chamberlain A. Bullfrog told me later, when we first-travelers related all this Valdez adventure history to the rest of the home gang:

"Good job. Can't gloss over the facts."

And Rudy Badger, who Chamberlain says is air-eh-dite, and please use the "eh" not the "you" like is common now but shouldn't be. Anyway, Rudy Badger said of this upcoming tragedy:

"Facts are stubbon things."

And Rudy Badger told me that was a famous quote by the Smothers Brothers or somebody.

Okay.

So we watched Riki and Mike, our two otter acquaintances, frolic about a hundred yards out and then this huge orca killer black and white raider shark whale, and his son or maybe ornimental woman orca friend, they rose up and smacked down on one, then the other. The band stopped. A couple little kids next to us blinked around cuz of the hush. Which descended itself over the adult crowd. And us.

I could tell Charlie wanted to do a that's-what-I'm-talking-about cheer but Folder gave him the stern eye. Like you do in church when someone drops a wafer-God-part on accident. Then the Old Man told us:

"Zotts idd. We're outta here. Rrright?"

And we all said right and we headed home.

Back Home

It was noon in the Big Field.

"Rrrefreshing change from ze cold, ja?" pointed out the Old Man.

We all rubbed our hands to like the warmth. Or I mean paws. And hands.

Crabby Crow was there, still mad about not touring with us. Also Chamberlain A. Bullfrog, who--surprises!--he decided he was up for traveling. To broaden the mind, he said.

"You wouldn't have liked it," Tosci the mouse told them both. "Cold. And we flew in a helicopter. It was jerky."

Tosci added that part for Chamberlain, who is land-based and avoids flying when he can. Of course, air travel is no big deal to Crabby Crow. But he doesn't like heat. Or cold. Which he still defended:

"I can take it."

Chamberlain the bullfrog then burped into the conversation with:

"Nevertheless, burr-up, consider me for your next historical foray. Of course land is preferred. Or better yet, sea."

"Velp," the Old Man scratched his chin, "I sink maybe ze aaairrrships, ja?"

"Airships?" we all asked. Cuz, okay, first we had a metal ship breakdown and now, made out of air? I don't think so.

"You want to float on air, go ahead," said Titus Fox wandering into our vicinity area.

"I don't believe, burr-up, a ship was ever made of air," stated Chamberlain A. Bullfrog. "Emperor's new clothes and so forth."

"Glass bottom boat," commented J.T. Woodchuck.

Which Titus Fox thought about thwapping him a good one but held off. Cuz glass has the property of air of see-through. So the answer was right in front of your eyes, only invisible.

"So it's a tourist boat!" I exclaimed, getting it. "Hmmm, but where. Or when."

"Or even How," tried Tosci.

"Nine, nine. Aeeiir ship," interrupted the Old Man. "Brimitive airplane, like ze Zeppelin."

"YOU NEED COOL AIR, WAY WAY DOWN INSIDE!" belted out Fat Charlie Chipmunk.

“Ja,” nodded the Old Man. “Zuper cool. State of ze art, way bock when. Und blush, zuper blush.”

“Blush?” asked Titus Fox. But Charlie beat the Old Man to that answer.

“Blush, beet red. In the early days, parents hated rock music which embarrassed the tool kids. Early pretend renegades. Back then.”

We all nodded, especially Tosci who exchanged a high five with Charlie on his a-stoot-ness of understanding wannabe post-stoneage rebels. But the Old Man clarified our issue. As always.

“Blush. Zuper comfy. Like ze tug-und-roll seats. Lay back und diggck idd!”

So . . . bottom line, after more deciphering of Old Man code words, we got the idea of our next trip being on airships of some sort which Chamberlain later told us were like giant balloons, color me clueless. And he said one balloon ship blew up bigtime and ended that modation of travel cuz of probably a billion law suits. So we had another smash-up to look forward to.

Then I broke that ice planning session by setting up a noon return party, loading my Red Flyer down with chips, crackers, cheeses, apples, Aquafina, plastic cokes, and those hard chocolate chips that Mom was ready to throw out.

We set it all up in the main meadow by the Old Gray Stump and even Slick the weasel entered into the proceedings with super high praise.

"Good to have you back," he murmured.

We all cheered.

- END -

More Turk Allcott

Keep up with Turk!

Check out all the other books, like:
Time Leak
Space Tweak
Shortcut . . . and others

Turk can be reached at turkallcott@gmail.com

www.ingramcontent.com/pod-product-compliance
Ingram Content Group UK Ltd.
Pitfield, Milton Keynes, MK11 3LW, UK
UKHW020217250726
13967UKWH00001B/44

9 781300 000235